Improving Intimacy

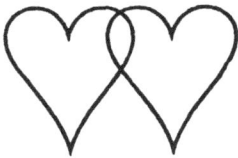

10 Powerful
Strategies

A Spiritual Approach

TOM O'CONNELL

Sanctuary

IMPROVING INTIMACY:
10 Powerful Strategies...
A Spiritual Approach

Published in the United States by
Sanctuary Unlimited
PO Box 25, Dennisport, MA 02639

Printed in U.S.A. First printing April 1993

For information, address:
Sanctuary, PO Box 25, Dennisport, MA 02639.

Library of Congress
Cataloging in Publication Data

O'Connell, Tom
Improving Intimacy: 10 Powerful Strategies

1. Intimacy 2. Love 3. Relationships
I. Title.
ISBN 0-9620318-2-8
Library of Congress
Catalog Card Number: 93-92664 CIP

Dedicated to the God of Love who is
always available to help us in our relationships;
with a special note of thanks to all who have
taught me how to expand my
own ability to give and receive love;
and sincere appreciation to Wendy
for her assistance
and enthusiastic support.

Order online at amazon.com

"Feeling understood is the only way an adult can be validated."
    -Psychologist ANNA ORNSTEIN

IMPROVING INTIMACY
10 Powerful Strategies (A spiritual approach)
by Tom O'Connell

1) A Look at Intimacy and Addiction

In today's world, the kind of closeness that many people describe as "intimacy" is actually addiction. But addiction impairs intimacy, so before we discuss the 10 powerful strategies for improving intimacy, we are going to look carefully at addictive relating.

Actually, one extremely important strategy for improving intimacy is to become more aware of our addictive tendencies and recover from them. Only then do we have a chance of achieving the kind of intimacy that enriches and helps to fulfill our lives.

First, let's look at the word "intimate," which comes from the Latin "intimus" and means "within," "private," "personal," "closely acquainted," or "very familiar."

Many people think intimacy is just another name for sexual intercourse. But the sexual act is only a part of intimacy. True intimacy is a blending of mind and spirit (and sometimes body) that goes beyond the sex act and brings us into unusual closeness to another human being. True intimacy is not achieved quickly. This labor of love takes time and demands respect for oneself and another. It's not a quick fix; it's an ongoing work of art.

Are you attached to your partner so strongly that you can't picture functioning without him? Are you so connected that you can't imagine living without her? Do you have habits that you perform with your partner? Are you preoccupied with your partner? Haunted by your partner? Lost in your partner? Easily disturbed by your partner? Caught in moods based on feelings about your mate?

If you have answered yes to any of these questions, there's a good chance that you are a relationship addict. And if you want to have healthy relationships you need to address your addictive tendencies. They impair your relationships, making healthy ones impossible to achieve, and form a triangle in which we are separated from our loved ones, our inner selves, and our God.

Don't take offense at the word "addict." It's a fine word, but many of us apply it mainly to drug addiction. The word "addict" means someone who is "devoted" to a "constant practice" or "habit." Most of us, at times, are relationship addicts. How about you?

2) Some Definitions to Consider

Basically, addiction is a condition of unhealthy dependence that impairs a person's ability to function to full potential. A very important problem we have when we're addicted is that we lose our ability to relate properly to another human being.

Another viewpoint of addiction is that it is a condition in which we will use any technique for adapting to the problems of life, other than healthy interpersonal relating. To lead a healthy life we need to learn to relate in healthy ways. But our addictive tendencies can be a serious barrier.

I think of addiction as Dependence with a Capital D. In a relationship when we are too dependent we are acting like an addict who is fixated on alcohol or drugs. A dependent person is in a state of suspense because when we're addicted we're left "hanging" much of the time.

When we are too dependent, it robs us of our freedom of choice when it comes to thoughts, words, actions and reactions. And freedom is a key element in building healthy relationships. Therefore, it's worth preserving and protecting.

3) FIVE Cs Of Relationship Addiction

If you're thinking you might be a relationship addict, reflect on the following factors. To help me remember them, I call them the Five Cs of addiction.

Addiction, or unhealthy Dependence, involves Craving, Compulsion, loss of one's Control despite attempts to control, and Continuation of the behavior even though there are life-damaging Consequences.

Do you find yourself Craving certain behaviors from your partner? Do you feel Compulsion driving you to get your own way? Do you feel like you are losing your Control at times? And do you Continue the behavior even though the Consequences are damaging to your life?

If you are caught in this kind of cycle, you are in a process involving more than just habit; you may qualify as an addict. But remember that the degree of intensity or harmfulness of addiction varies from person to person. The dividing line between habit and addictive tendency is not easy to pin down.

4) The O/C Of Relationship Addiction

Are you addicted or not? To find out, take a close look at what I call the O/C of addiction, Obsession and Compulsion. If you are haunted by the object of your addiction, preoccupied with thoughts of it, you are experiencing Obsession. Do you feel irresistibly drawn toward some particular behavior? And are you impulsive about it? Do you feel compelled to act? If you feel driven, that is Compulsion. Obsession and Compulsion are at the heart of every addiction, and if you can relate to what I'm saying here, consider that you may be more addicted to your partner than in a state of healthy love.

5) PMESS of Relationship Addiction

Relationships involve our whole being, whether we realize it or not, and addiction also affects us in all of our aspects whether they be Physical, Mental,

Emotional, Social, or Spiritual. Relating affects our bodies, minds, emotions, social activity, and spiritual journey. So a healthy relationship is a good medicine for our whole being; and an unhealthy one is poison. But when we are used to taking in addictive poison over a long period of time there are certain responses that are common. I call them the DDT&W.

6) DDT&W of Relationship Addiction

As we round out this very brief course in the key factors that appear in addictive relating, let's look at the DDT&W, which may sound a bit like a corporate name but stands for Defense, Denial, Tolerance, and Withdrawal. Each of these four factors is found in unhealthy dependence. They can be called hallmarks of addictive disease, whether the problem involves alcohol, drugs, food, gambling, or relationships.

Defense
It is human to Defend our behavior once we have chosen a course of action. When we're addicted to another person we have turned over our inner power to an outside force that is doing our choosing for us. But we still want to think we're calling the shots. So we are likely to use phrases such as these: "I can handle the relationship." "I've got things under control." "The good things outweigh the bad." "The sex is so good!" "There's pain but there's comfort,

too." "I think there's definitely going to be a change for the better."

Denial

Denial is also a trait that accompanies addiction. It's an attempt to shield myself from the shock I must face if I square off and recognize the truth that will pressure me to make changes in my life that I'd rather not make. If you try to persuade me to believe I'm in an unhealthy relationship, I may simply say: "That's ridiculous." "You don't know what you're talking about." "There are a lot of people worse off than I am." "You don't know the whole story."

I may refuse to admit my problem, no matter how obvious it may be to you. And my Denial may include outright lying and manipulative behavior. It can even involve limiting the amount of contact, similar to the way an alcoholic may attempt to measure the number of drinks. Also, we can deceive ourselves, and claim we are only hurting ourselves a little, not a lot. This is sometimes called minimizing.

Tolerance

Tolerance is another important factor that goes with addiction. In simple language, it means that we need increasingly more of our object of devotion to get the originally desired effect. Our bodies and minds adapt to our behavior; our responses change, and sometimes our Tolerance may build to a level at which the original sensation can't be reproduced.

This is not only true of drug effects, it's also true of sexual effects and other behaviors that accompany addictive relating.

Withdrawal

The W in DDT&W refers to the Withdrawal symptoms that happen when we try to quit an addiction. After stopping our addictive behavior, we are faced with unpleasant symptoms: "I think I'll die!" "I can't live without him!" "I need her!"

Among the unpleasant Physical symptoms are sweating, cramps, and even tremors. Mental and emotional symptoms include feelings of impending doom, insecurity, mood swings, anger, isolation, depression, and confusion. Spiritual withdrawal symptoms include despair, loss of hope, anger with God, a basic dissatisfaction with life, a feeling of powerlessness, and a loss of confidence.

The pain of relationship withdrawal is similar to grieving over a death.

7) The CPF Of Relationship Addiction

Addiction also has a CPF factor. It is Chronic, Progressive, and potentially Fatal. Yet some people seem able to maintain a steadily destructive holding pattern without escalating the harmful course of events over a long period. The Chronic nature of relationship addiction is similar to other addictions in that it is an ongoing problem.

Just as there are many kinds of chronic alcoholics such as those who are daily drinkers, weekend drinkers, and periodic binge drinkers, relationship addicts may be involved in unhealthy, addictive relationships daily, weekly, or even less frequently. But in any case, the problem is Chronic.

Looking at the Progressive aspect of relationship addiction, usually the relationship deteriorates over time while causing untold pain and suffering.

The Fatal possibilities include suicide, homicide, and using other hazardous addictions to cope with the pain. There is another kind of fatality too, when we carry around with us the emotional death that happens when we persist in staying with a failed and toxic addictive relationship. My belief is that God did not intend us to be functioning like zombies.

8) Attempting To Fill Inner Emptiness

Addiction, whether we are discussing unhealthy relationships with people, alcohol, drugs, betting, or food, involves a continuing attempt to fill an inner emptiness or relieve inner discomfort by turning to some behavior that will bring the sense of fulfillment or comfort we are looking for. The relief is always temporary, and to be free we must pay a price.

It takes courage to choose pain in order to find freedom from addiction. But it's worth the effort to free ourselves, and there's a special bonus. When we choose healthy instead of addictive relating, we access a level of happiness beyond description.

9) The Three Basic Relationships

In this discussion I am emphasizing the addictive relating that goes on between two committed people who are trying to live full lives together. But it's important to realize that there is more to life than relating to just one other person, in a couple.

There are three key relationships to concern ourselves with in life: the relationship with self, the relationship to others, and the relationship to God.

When all three relationships are in balance, we achieve a wonderful wholeness. Each relationship, healthy or unhealthy, affects the others, and to focus on one of the three to the exclusion of the others leads to serious problems. Balance is the key.

10) The Process of Addictive Relating

Addictive relating, as with other addictions, is a process that begins with the choice of a love object, or object of devotion, that makes us feel good or lessens our discomfort with life. We move from habit to unhealthy dependence, and finally to addiction. At that point we lose our freedom to choose what is best for ourselves.

Obsessed by our love object, we are preoccupied or haunted by thoughts about the person. Becoming compulsive, we feel driven to actions designed to achieve our desires. Irresistibly drawn by the power of our chosen love object, we lose power over ourselves. That's why they call it "falling in love."

When we "fall" out of balance we are in danger, and even though true love is a wonderful thing, addictive love that masquerades as true love can lead us to disaster.

In this painful process we exhibit the Five Cs of addiction as we become caught up in a cycle of intensity that involves Craving, Compulsion, loss of Control, and Continuation of the unhealthy behavior despite life-damaging Consequences. Caught in a web of powerful thoughts and feelings that affect us physically, mentally, emotionally, socially and spiritually, we defend our behavior, deny it, and suffer from the tolerance factor, meaning we need more and more of our love object. And we experience painful withdrawal symptoms when we cannot get what we desire.

Finally, we find ourselves in the CPF of addiction as we become diseased by our chronic, progressive behaviors that tend to worsen with time and may lead us to fatal outcomes.

Now that we know how addictive we can be, we are in a position to take steps toward recovery, and start practicing real intimacy.

First, though, we need to take a look at what intimacy is all about:

Love!

11) Some Thoughts About Infatuation

Many people mistake infatuation for love, and the word comes from the Latin "infatuatio" meaning "foolish." Dictionary language tells us that when we become infatuated we are "thoroughly under the influence of foolish passion; acting without sense or reason."

We are attracted, like travelers in the desert, to the "ignis fatuus," or "foolish fire," which is a false light or illusion. The real thing would be a nurturing campfire.

Infatuation is a state of mind that's a bit like being in love with love. The self-identified great addict St. Augustine, who chased love passionately, said, "I loved not yet, yet I loved to love...I sought that I might love, in love with loving."

12) Healthy Relating

Healthy relationships are based on a foundation of unselfish love, not on the false light of infatuation or the pursuit of pleasure. To live is to need to connect, and "relate" means "connect." But our challenge is to connect with another in a balanced, not addictive, way.

Also, we must remember that our partner shouldn't be expected to fulfill all of our insatiable needs. After all, our perceived "needs" are subject to changes based on moods and desires which are very unpredictable and basically self-centered.

Self-centered expectations are the very stuff that leads to addictive relating and deteriorating relationships. If we act out our desire to connect in the same way we approach our use of alcohol and other addictive love objects, we feel good briefly, feel unfulfilled the rest of the time, and are about as close to understanding love as Columbus was to reaching the Orient.

Romantic love is by nature exhilarating, and operates like cocaine, with a series of highs followed by a series of crashes, and no real middle ground. Yet the middle ground is where love lives. In the middle ground we will sacrifice a perceived need for the sake of the one we love. And we will learn to think of our needs as "preferences."

With healthy love, "Enough is enough." With addictive love, "More is better." There's nothing wrong with romance, but expecting a relationship to be always romantic is a form of unbalanced thinking. And so is the notion that our "highs" are "needs."

13) Some Thoughts on Love

Love is an art that few have mastered, I believe, and it's a subject that fascinates and mystifies me. I don't pretend to be an expert at it, just a serious student. And it's important for us to become students of love because love doesn't just "happen." We make it, and we can decide to dissolve it.

In my lifetime I have had a variety of theme songs about love. One of my favorites was "Send in the Clowns." Yet at other times I was haunted by the romance of "Love is a Many Splendored Thing."

In search of love, many of us thought we had found it, and then we lost it, and there we were with our heads shaking back and forth, wondering what had happened to us. Then we went through the grieving process after parting with a partner, and once again there we were in the arena of life with questions on who to connect with, and how to do it.

14) Sex and Wholeness

When the time became right to connect again, many of us got involved in too much too soon. We were like the camel in the desert who, after spending much time with great thirst, started to swig in all the water in the oasis. It was too much for us. And it was not true intimacy because the emphasis was too much on the sensual instead of the spiritual.

In Latin, the word "sex" means "to cut." I wonder if this goes back to an ancient concept that one person was cut in half, with one part male (Adam) and the other female (Eve). Destined to come together as Adam and Eve, they were two separate yet united beings.

In a caring relationship, the halves are rejoined physically, psychologically, and spiritually, which includes much more than repetitive acts of sexual intercourse. In a relationship a new entity is created, a kind of new being.

I think this rejoined state, this reunion of halves, is that natural state of wholeness we are striving for in our intimate relationships. It's a state in which two halves add up to more than one whole. And it's a state of living, or lifestyle, that can be liberating, maturing and fulfilling.

15) The Various Kinds of Love

There are many viewpoints on love, but I have a special fondness for the description C. S. Lewis used in a book called The Four Loves, where he discusses affection, friendship, Eros and charity.

"Affection," says Lewis, is modest and familiar, ordinary and easy, like "old clothes" that get more comfortable the more often you wear them. This kind of love involves give and take, fairness and decency.

"Friendship" is appreciative love, and involves common interests, he suggests. It's when we see the same truth, accept each other for ourselves, share our mutual respect, and develop understanding.

"Eros" brings a preoccupation with the beloved, Lewis observes. Erotic love, which is more intense than friendship, wants the whole person, not just the sex act, and Lewis says it enters into a relationship "like an invader." Passions soar and "pleasure pushed to its extreme, shatters us like pain." There are pledges of "true love" and there is "idol worship." Obviously, at this point our addictive tendencies can escalate dramatically.

"Charity" is on yet another level. Lewis says it involves "practicing the presence of God," and he emphasizes that in this kind of love there are "no safe investments." It's unconditional love!

Charity is the kind of love that St. Paul was so beautifully describing in I Corinthians 13: "Love is patient and kind; it is not jealous or conceited or proud; love is not ill-mannered or selfish or irritable; love does not keep a record of wrongs; love is not happy with evil, but is happy with the truth. Love never gives up; and its faith, hope, and patience never fail...."

A healthy intimate relationship of the best type will include each of these kinds of love, at one time or another, and sometimes they will overlap.

16) Real Love

What is real love? It's mysterious and defies rigid defining, but you know it when you have it in your heart. And you know its joy whether you are giving or receiving it.

I greatly appreciate the way psychologist Harry Stack Sullivan chose to describe love. "When the satisfaction or security of another person becomes as significant as your own...a state of love exists."

Then there is Erich Fromm's belief that love is a decision to "know, care, respond, respect...." The word "respect" means to "look at." How many people are willing to truly look at each other in mutual respect as whole persons?

Fromm views real love as an art form requiring discipline, concentration, patience, concern with mastery, faith, courage, and activity. These are the same ingredients we need when we try to master any behavior. Imagine the results throughout the world if we were all willing to work at love as a way of life that demands the best we have to give.

C.S. Lewis emphasizes that "to love is to be vulnerable." He also says promiscuous sex is like chewing things and then spitting them out again.

I once heard some unforgettable words about love and connectedness from psychologist Anna Ornstein: "Feeling understood is the only way an adult can be validated." How are we able to validate, or love, one another? We do it through empathy, not through the addictive pursuit of pleasure. Ornstein defines "empathy" as the ability "to realize and understand another person's feelings, needs and suffering."

Empathy is the opposite of indifference, which hurts and shrivels us. Empathy heals and expands both giver and receiver. And it is a very important ingredient in what we call "love."

We need empathy for ourselves...and for others.

17) Love and Self-Discipline

One of the problems with our yearning to connect is that it brings on feelings that are very powerful and can easily move us into addictive behaviors. We can become overwhelmed by our own obsessive thinking and worrying, and exhausted by compulsive actions based on fear. Fear of not getting what we want, or fear of losing what we already have.

Instead of being caught up in fear, we need to extend ourselves for another person's benefit and discipline those inner urges of ours that can't be fully satisfied in this existence. We have to learn how to defer gratification. To really experience joy in eating ice cream, we need to learn to lick it slowly instead of swallowing it in four bites that send jabs of pain into our skulls. And instead of eating the blossoms on the apple tree we should have the patience to wait for the fruit to ripen. It's worth the wait.

True love is not the continual satisfaction of appetites, it is the willingness to commit ourselves to another while not losing ourselves in the process. To do that, we need to be disciplined. Also, we need to invest time and energy in our partner, not expecting an instant return. We have to be willing to set aside our own desires when we do the dance of intimacy.

To accomplish this, we must be fully ourselves and allow our partner to be a complete person too. A loving relationship is not an event, not a destination; it's a journey filled with unexpected daily adventures.

18) The Need to Grow Together

In the journey of intimacy, before we can extend ourselves in a loving relationship with another, we need to know and love ourselves well. We have to be aware of our strengths and our weaknesses; and we need to accept the other's need to experience self-awareness and personal growth too.

If we are a dependent type and can't live a full life alone, we are unlikely to be able to learn how to live a full life with another. Although we can help each other to grow toward our destinies, the journey of life is basically individual And that's where love comes into the picture. It isn't easy to treasure our partner's separateness when it conflicts with our desire for closeness. But love includes elements of self-discipline and the willingness to sacrifice self.

John Donne wrote: "We are alone together, you and I, and we cannot make each other unalone." Yet we can help, nurture, and express love to each other by encouraging freedom to be oneself, with our gifts and defects. When two people relate together and look beyond the defects, appreciate the gifts, and practice being supportive, that's love in operation.

In true love we embrace all of the elements of relating, both the peak experiences of union and the shattering experiences of loss and loneliness. That's where the development of our emotional balance becomes critically important. And it's well worth the continuing effort. Two people united in love, and dedicated to a healthy relationship, can achieve a level of happiness that is beyond description.

In the Chinese Book of Changes the harmony of such a healthy intimate relationship is expressed in these words: "True joy is the harmony between two people's essential selves." This nurturing harmony involves "sincerity, truth and goodness." With such harmony, a relationship truly blossoms.

The I Ching also notes that when joy is not your goal you are more apt to find it. Love, when chased, is like the elusive butterfly. But if we concentrate on giving love we will attract love like a magnet. It's an old idea, but ancient wisdom has stood the test of time and is valuable to us in our spiritual journey. The concept that it is better to give than receive is a powerful one. And its truth can be our guide.

19) Key Elements in the 10 Strategies

It's a challenge to condense the many possible interpretations of love and intimacy into 10 simple strategies. But I believe that the millions of words used throughout history on this subject can be boiled down to 10 basic principles.

Also, I feel that when discussing how to improve love and intimacy skills, the hazards of addictive relating must be stressed. Addictive relating is a real barrier to harmony in partnerships, and a key issue that deserves ongoing attention in the development and maintenance of healthy intimate relationships.

As an antidote to toxic, addictive relating I stress the importance of developing a spiritual focus in all relationships. Spirituality is the key to successful relating and healthy intimacy.

20) The 10 Powerful Strategies

1) **Become a student of intimate relating.**
2) **Recover from your addictive relating.**
3) **Develop a spiritual basis for loving.**
4) **Learn to love, not compete or control.**
5) **Learn to listen and listen to learn.**
6) **Communicate your feelings and ideas.**
7) **Resolve conflict in healthy ways.**
8) **Give appreciation generously.**
9) **Become who you really are and love it.**
10) **Intimacy is a dance, so let's dance!**

These strategies could be the subjects of ten books. But reading has limits; and living actively is what life is all about. So we need to test what we read and see how useful it is in actual practice.

These ten strategies are not designed to bring you a perfect relationship. Perfection is not the goal. Relating in a loving, caring way is the goal, and that involves a lifetime journey. But the practice of these useful strategies will enhance your ability to enjoy life more fully on a daily basis.

As a student of intimacy, you will learn and grow, and each of your close relationships will give you opportunities to improve your intimacy skills.

Now let's look at each of the ten strategies...

#1...Become A Student of Intimate Relating

Intimate relating is an art form, and works of art aren't created by dabbling. We have to practice our art consistently. Since creating healthy relationships, or "connecting," is the essence of life itself and not just a small part of life, it requires our best efforts.

Lectures and books may be useful, and therapists may be helpful when we get stuck, but our best teachers are the people with whom we connect. People we live with are challenging teachers, but our associates in various organizations can also teach us. We all need to study intimacy in every relationship, whether at home, at work, or elsewhere.

We need to practice what we learn, and learn from our practice. And it requires humility to realize that our higher education in intimate relating brings no diploma that certifies our expertise. Intimacy is an academy for lifelong learning where we all take turns playing the roles of teacher and student.

#2...Recover From Your Addictive Relating

The most harmful barrier to healthy relating is addiction. And that includes the whole range of addictions to toxic substances and behaviors, plus relationship addiction itself. We have explored this subject already, but here I want to reiterate that in our three key relationships--to self, others and God-- our addictive tendencies separate us from the honest, straightforward relationships that can bring us to emotional balance and wholeness.

Addiction alienates; alienation renders intimate relating impossible. In recovery, when people trace their addictions back to the starting point, they usually find problems of self-love and self-esteem. To come to grip with these issues I recommend the mutual help approach used in the spiritually-based Twelve Step groups where kindred spirits meet, share truth in an atmosphere of unconditional love, and heal themselves so they may become ready for healthy relating.

Relating is not simple. It involves responsibility, limits, and consequences brought on by our behavior. And mutual help groups provide an excellent testing ground for practicing new healthy behaviors.

If you think you have no addictions to address, and no unhealthy behaviors to part with, I suggest that you may be prone to self-righteousness, tunnel vision, or maybe perfectionism. But there are mutual help groups that address those issues too.

Everyone should be in a mutual help group. Nobody has to become addicted to learn to relate properly, but it helps. That's because the addictions lead us into recovery groups where we then receive advanced character training and values clarification. Join a group! It will help you and your relationships, and will give you a network of support in the good times, and when you have relationship problems.

#3...Develop a Spiritual Basis for Loving

Love is a spiritual mystery that resists our feeble attempts to analyze it. Although love may involve the brain at times, it is basically from the heart. And the heart, I believe, is where God lives in each of us. The ancient Egyptians, when they were preparing a dead person for the afterlife, flushed the brain down the drain but carefully preserved the heart because they were convinced that it was the most important organ and the home of the human spirit.

To love is to be spiritual, and we must not let our brains take over the process of relating and dictate to our hearts. A friend of mine once said to me, "The heart has reasons that reason knows nothing about." I believe she was right.

Ideally, we should be guided by wisdom, which is the perfect blend of intelligence and love. But no matter how intelligent we are, we can't reason our way to loving because love is not reasonable. Yet we can use our minds to help us learn the principles of what to do and what not to do when relating. And then our hearts will not be misguided by the faulty logic that often comes from our brains.

From a spiritual perspective, intimate relating is a blending of two spirits in which your life and my life become our life, even though we maintain our precious individuality. When this happens, a new spiritual entity is born. To nourish and nurture that new spiritual entity called "us," I believe constant mutual spiritual growth and development are vital.

This is not a new concept. Since ancient times, the notion of partnership based on spiritual unity has been common. And in our times I believe we need a massive return to this approach to relating. When my basic goal in our relationship is to nourish and uplift you spiritually, and your goal is the same for me, all other things are destined to fall into place quite harmoniously.

If the spirit is right, and the relationship of each person to God is right, then the physical as well as the psychological aspects of the relationship will be worked out in a loving and satisfying way. And the result will be "connecting" at the deepest levels.

When my relationship with you includes praying for you and wishing you well in all your endeavors, and encouraging you to develop your own spiritual being while we develop our intimate relationship, that certainly is love.

It's also love when I pray regularly to God for my own spiritual growth and meditate daily to unite myself with the will of God and His peace. My own growth will certainly bring my partner blessings too.

What I am saying here is that my ideal for the ultimate relationship on this planet is one in which two partners love each other deeply while also loving God as the third and Supreme Force in the relationship. Their love for God will not separate them from each other. And their love for each other will not separate them from God. The two, bonded together in sacred intimacy, operating beyond selfishness and addiction, will be one with God. And that is the most wonderful gift known to humanity.

With no spiritual basis for love, there is no basis at all, because love and spirituality are one and the same. So nourish that spirituality, and work on that spiritual basis, and your love will steadily grow...and grow...and grow.

#4...Learn to Love, not Compete or Control

Love doesn't compete and it doesn't control. It frees. It nurtures. It gives. It receives. It celebrates and it listens. It shares. It cares. It laughs. It cries. It expresses and it trusts. It meets you. It's there for you. It risks. It opens itself. It discloses and it affirms. It validates. It understands. It knows you. It protects. It respects and it encourages. It touches. It heals. It commits. And it grows with you.

Love is a work of art created through discipline and concentration; patience and kindness; concern and faith; courage and activity; detachment, looking beyond faults, and meeting needs.

Love doesn't need to compete, and it rests comfortably in its own essence. It doesn't want to beat anybody or win anything. It doesn't want what you have. It isn't in a race. It's not driven by anxiety. And it may exhibit passion, but it is not obsessed or compulsive. It prefers cooperation to competition.

Love doesn't need to control. It has no interest in dominating anybody or determining anyone else's existence. It knows that the only control necessary in life is self-control; and that challenge is enough to keep it very busy working on purifying its own heart.

Love does not need to possess or own you. It combines strength and gentleness. It gives affection without demanding or complaining. It makes room for mistakes. It may confront, but it doesn't need to force issues. It tells the truth, but its aim is not to hurt or harm. It is filled with empathy for all.

Love is a gift from God which He put into all creation. We have an abundance of it available to us. And the more we give it away the more of it comes to us. The supply is infinite because God's love for us has no limits. So don't waste your energy competing and controlling. Use your energy on useful pursuits, like expanding your own ability to love.

#5...Learn to Listen and Listen to Learn

Vast numbers of people seem to have no interest in truly listening to others. They are self-centered in what they say and impatient to say it. They are concerned mainly with their own thoughts. They haven't learned to listen with heightened awareness.

To respect, or "look at" another person, we have to listen carefully. Not just for the words. But for the sounds of the words too. Words may convey what we are thinking, but our sounds transmit what we feel.

Listening well is one of the most important tools for achieving intimacy. It means setting oneself aside and letting another disclose truth. It means not letting the thoughts stray while the other person is talking. It means trying to understand what is being said and why it is being said. It means dropping all resistance to the other person's communication. It means truly being there, fully present, not distracted by thoughts of the past or the future. Listening is difficult! That's why it's so precious to us when we are close to someone who knows how to do it.

All too often in couples, one is a compulsive talker and one is a reluctant listener, and there's no truly honest communication going on between them. The self-centered talker gives lectures and vents frustrations, while the self-centered listener engages in selective listening. The result? A waste of the energy expended by both self-centered people.

The compulsive talker needs to talk less, be more thoughtful when talking, and expand the amount of time given to concentrated listening. The reluctant listener needs to do more talking, share honestly, and learn to listen with an attitude of enthusiasm.

We all need to keep working on our listening skills. And that's not easy when you're under stress or tired. But when we listen better we learn more about the spiritual beings around us, our fellow humans, and we learn to love better too. Are you interested in becoming a person who practices love? Then you have to refine your listening skills. So do it! And don't forget to do it! Learn to listen and listen to learn.

#6...Communicate Your Feelings and Ideas

Communication is vitally important in sustaining an intimate relationship, and it requires quality time. Don't just plan to have time to talk when you get around to it; make it a priority in your life. Explore ideas, identify feelings, and discuss your reality with your partner. Work from a basis of mutual trust, and realize that intimate communication is a true growth experience.

If you don't already practice it, learn the art of intimate, back-and-forth, in-depth conversation. Try to be spontaneous. When expressing yourself, be open and honest, and let the conversation flow from one topic to another on its own. Also, avoid giving speeches and "dumping" all of your problems onto your partner's mind. Your partner is not a dump site.

When feelings are expressed, remind yourself that feelings are not debatable. They're not right or wrong. They're just feelings. So please never say to your partner, "You shouldn't feel that way." That invalidates the truth of your loved one's being, and such behavior is in very poor taste.

Your partner's statements about feelings are an expression of inner reality, and nobody has the right to negate another's inner truth. We must respect our partner's feelings and not criticize them. Also, if our partner's actions move us to give some constructive criticism, we need to avoid doing it in public. The guideline is: "Criticize in private; praise in public."

We also have to watch out for black-and-white, all-or-nothing extremes of thinking. And we need to avoid generalizing because our absolute statements just don't jibe with reality. And we have to learn to dwell on the positive, not the negative, and avoid any tendency to belittle our partner's statements just because we don't happen to agree with them. Your partner is a free, responsible individual with a right to opinions. And please don't forget that!

Other important stances to avoid in conversation are the positions of superiority or inferiority, whether stated or unstated. Intimacy is a dance of two equal partners, with no fixed leader. Or we might say that the partners take turns being leader.

Think of conversation as an adventure in foreign territory, a trip into the unknown. Have fun when you communicate with your loved one, but also make an effort to be courteous and thoughtful about your partner's ideas and feelings. Remember that your adventures in communication are an important part of your journey through life. And they are a vital ingredient in your relationship.

#7...Resolve Conflict in Healthy Ways

In a partnership of equals, when a conflict arises it doesn't have to turn into a nasty battle royal. And here are some tactics to avoid. Avoid jumping to conclusions, and don't think you're able to read your partner's mind. Encourage open, full expression, and avoid quick negative responses. Also, don't make up predictions based on your idea of what your partner may be thinking. In the name of humility, you need to acknowledge that although God may know your partner's thoughts, you are not a mind reader.

You should avoid exaggerating the meaning of what your partner says, and avoid minimizing it too. Use the "I" word as much as possible when you are working out a conflict, and keep the "you" word to a minimum. But realize that both words are useful at times. Why sidestep the reality that "you" have done something that presses my buttons? The "I feel" statement can be overdone!

Stick to the issues at hand too, and define areas of responsibility in your relationship so there won't be confusion. Don't contradict your partner either, or use "Yes-but" responses to suggestions. And take a "time out" if you find the discussion getting heated. In my opinion, unleashed hostility is not therapeutic; is not appropriate in dialogue designed to resolve conflict; and it can easily lead to verbal or physical violence which has no place in loving relationships.

In dialogue we don't want to intentionally hurt our partner even though we may disagree on certain items. And we don't engage in name-calling, or the blame game. Also, we don't label our partner as a "jerk" or "loser" just because he or she won't come around to our way of thinking.

It's also helpful not to use too many "advice" words like "should," "must," or "have to." It's best to limit advice to responses to requests for it. And remember that we don't have to win out in dialogue. The point of it all is to promote understanding and move toward positive action, not to defeat somebody.

Communication isn't a strategy for getting our own way. It's about loving and being patient, kind, courteous, and considerate. When we communicate to resolve conflict with our partner, it's an act of love requiring courage. Avoiding conflict is sometimes useful in keeping the peace, but can also be a form of cowardice. Healthy dialogue is difficult to practice, and challenging, but it is definitely worth the effort.

#8...Give Appreciation Generously

In dialogue, remember that your partner is a very special person who deserves the best you have to give. And his or her role in life is not to grant all your wishes. Your partner's special qualities deserve appreciation, and the appreciation we feel needs to be expressed. Taking a loved one's special qualities for granted is a form of neglect. We have to learn to express our appreciation openly, honestly, and often.

We each should encourage our partner toward reaching maximum potential, and invite sharing of thoughts and feelings. We should support with praise and encouragement, praise and reassure, strive to give our partner a sense of security, or sanctuary, and avoid powerplays. Intimacy is not about power; it's about closeness, and connection, and love.

One way to express love is remembering "little things" our partner enjoys. Generosity shouldn't end with the early phase of getting to know one another. Genuine interest in and concern about our partner should be ongoing. And we should never forget the little gifts, including a smile or cheerful word, along with the affectionate use of our partner's name which is each person's treasured possession.

So stay aware of your partner's special qualities, and do express your gratitude. Be friendly to your partner. Rejoice in your partner's success. Share in your partner's grief. And always remember to give appreciation generously.

#9...Become Who You Really Are and Love It

Our journey through life is both inner and outer. It's the life of our minds and hearts, the life we live with others, and the life in which we relate to the Power who created us. It's a relationship journey involving self, others, and God. And more than anything else, it's a journey of self-discovery.

Inside of us there is a person trying to emerge. This person can be compared to the pearl inside the oyster, the treasure in the cave, the lotus in the mud, or the diamond in the dust. But no matter how we try to describe that inner being, it's a mystery that each of us must work on, one day at a time, one moment at a time, throughout our lives.

Some psychologists call our journey through life a quest for wholeness; others describe it with terms such as "self-actualization"; and others use words such as "individuation." Each view has merit.

We need to become whole, which doesn't mean perfect. It means that we heal our wounds and our brokenness and become one being instead of split or fragmented. If we actualize ourselves, we are getting in touch with our destiny and bringing out that inner person and making it real instead of hiding it. And when we individuate we are coming to terms with our reality, our talents, our abilities, our potential.

In other words, we are becoming who we really are. And I believe that who we really are amounts to the stupendous fact that each of us is a special child of a loving God who presides over our lives with an attitude of unconditional love, and encourages us to experience life fully. The loving God I believe in does not stop loving us when we make mistakes, and passes on to us as gifts our own wonderful, God-given capacities for truth and love.

But we must take those capacities out of the oyster, out of the cave, out of the mud, out of the dust, and use them for our good, the good of others, and the good of God's divine plan for this planet.

Accepting ourselves as we really are, we take responsibility not only for our actions but for our thoughts, words and reactions. And we try to rise beyond negativity, looking for the good instead of the unwholesome. We respect our bodies which are temples of our spirits, and we choose appropriate relaxation, rest, exercise and food. As we increase the frequency of extending ourselves toward others, we are less self-centered in our relationships.

Instead of chasing immediate gratification, we learn to choose temporary discomfort. Why? Because we accept the truth that the object of our deep desire is often not appropriate for our growth. We become enthusiastic about growth experiences even though they often bring us pain. We value our expanding ability to communicate our ideas and feelings. We try to express appreciation for life throughout each day. And, as we pray and meditate on a daily basis, we improve our relationships with self, others, and God. And we achieve a valuable perspective on the meaning of the word "intimacy."

At this point, have we arrived at our destination? No. We've simply arrived at the awareness of who we are and what a wonder this life is. And having become aware of who we are, it becomes clear that we no longer need to try to run from ourselves into addictive practices.

Instead of a frantic search for God outside of ourselves, we practice the presence of God within us and in our own lives. And we learn to love ourselves and others as reflections of the Divine Spirit who brought us into being. This brings us peace and joy beyond description. And it certainly improves our capacity for intimacy.

#10...Intimacy is a Dance, so Let's Dance!

When we reach the stage of self-realization, or enlightenment, we accept and love ourselves as we really are and as we can become. We learn to enjoy who we are and who others are. With humility, we develop a sense of humor about our weaknesses. And in this attitude of self-love we move out beyond ourselves to accept and love others.

At some point in the journey we realize that God has infinite love for us and all creation. And then, having had a powerful inner experience of God, we start relating to God, who lives in our hearts as well as outside of us, as our kind, compassionate, loving parent and closest friend.

Along the way, we get in touch with our real needs and are willing to ask to have them met. We go beyond ourselves and make safe places where others can share life with us; and we show concern for their needs. We know what we feel, and we share our feelings. We recognize patterns of behavior that are not fulfilling, and we become willing to change them. We learn to think straight, talk straight, act straight, and truly connect with others. And we learn to be patient in times of conflict and discomfort.

We begin to have more realistic expectations about ourselves as well as others. Since entertaining resentment squanders our energy, we don't waste our time that way. As dialogue works miracles of healing and understanding, we become students of it.

In this growth process, we avoid becoming driven by our feelings, and also learn not to "sit" with them excessively. Instead, we identify our feelings, observe them, learn from them, and moderate them.

Sharing becomes a way of life, and we do it with our partner. We also develop support systems where kindred spirits help each other on the steep, ecstasy-producing ascents up the mountain, and during the anxiety-producing slides down into the valleys.

We learn new skills for living. We give up old unhealthy habits. We engage in self-exploration as an ongoing practice. We improve our basic attitudes, striving always for the positive. And we relish the ability and the opportunity to grow into the persons we were designed to be: reflections of a loving God.

We come to realize that a comment attributed to Abraham Lincoln certainly makes a lot of sense, and can help us transform our lives: "Most folks are as happy as they make up their minds to be."

We eventually choose to use more energy giving love than seeking it, while at the same time learning to accept it graciously when it comes our way. And then we start to understand the power of the prayer of St. Francis of Assisi:

Peace Prayer

"Lord, make me an instrument of your peace. Where there is hatred, let me sow love; where there is discord, harmony; where there is injury, pardon; where there is error, truth; where there is doubt, faith; where there is despair, hope; where there is darkness, light; where there is sadness, joy.

"O Divine Master, grant that I may not so much seek: to be consoled, as to console; to be understood, as to understand; to be loved, as to love; for it is in giving, that we receive; it is in forgetting self, that we find ourselves; it is in pardoning, that we are pardoned; and it is in dying, that we are born to eternal life."

I interpret the word "dying" as parting with our egotistical selfishness and beginning a new life based on the spirit of love. When this transition from a wintry inner landscape shifts to the grandeur of spring's blossoming, we celebrate life, and truth, and most of all, we celebrate our ability to love.

By applying ourselves to the task of personal growth, we have developed an ability to join the dance of intimacy. We have learned how to move lightly, and spin, and slide, and whirl. We have learned how to set our partner free, and then treasure our partner's presence when we touch again.

We have learned that control, other than self-control, has no place in this dance. And we know now that real spontaneity and love are vital to this rhythmic way of relating. So we embrace the dance of intimacy, and we dance.

A dance is a fluid thing, like a river or a stream, but it doesn't have a destination. It exists for its own sake, for its own joy. As we practice the 10 powerful strategies for improving intimacy, using a spiritual approach, we are not operating as students working toward a certificate or degree. We are more like self-educated students who experience the flow of life and learn from it.

We will not become experts. Nor will we become masters of intimacy. We will simply remain students as we continue our journey, doing the best we can to practice love of self, others, and God. And in a way we had never dreamed possible, we will find that our capacity for intimacy has expanded to include all the people we touch. Finally, we will learn the meaning of joy. And we will be in awe of the mystery of it all.

I wish you joy in your journey!

NOTE...

Next I am including some thoughts for you to ponder...from this text, and elsewhere. Then, for the rest of the book, I am providing some space where you may wish to reflect on observations in these pages that triggered deep thinking.

You may even wish to go through the book a second time, reading more slowly, and noting on the "reflection" pages the thoughts that have become important to you.

Writing from our hearts can reinforce our resolve to make changes in our lives. So I encourage you to do a little scribbling.

SOME OF MY FAVORITE THOUGHTS

**Healthy relationships are based on
unselfish love.**

Real love brings joy to giver and receiver.

**Empathy heals and expands giver and
receiver.**

**If we concentrate on giving love
we will attract love.**

**Our best teachers are those
with whom we are intimate.**

**Love and spirituality
are one and the same.**

Love doesn't need to control or compete.

Intimacy is a dance of equal partners.

**Each of us is a special child
of a loving God.**

**When joy is not your goal you are
more apt to find it--I Ching**

SOME OF MY FAVORITE THOUGHTS

Love one another--Jesus

Cease desire--Buddha

Know thyself--Oracle at Delphi

**I suffer most because of
me and selfishness--Lao-Tzu**

**Lord, make me an instrument
of your peace--St. Francis of Assisi**

When in doubt, just love.

Thoughts to reflect on...

Thoughts to reflect on...

Thoughts to reflect on...

Thoughts to reflect on...

Improving Intimacy 50

Thoughts to reflect on...

Thoughts to reflect on...

.

Thoughts to reflect on...

Thoughts to reflect on...

About the Author

Tom O'Connell, a Cape Cod resident, is a health writer, lecturer, and author of the popular Cape Cod Times advice column, "On Addiction." At Cape Cod Community College he teaches writing and designed the course, "Creating Healthy Relationships." He is listed in *Who's Who in the East*.

Memberships include Cape Cod Writers' Center; New England Chapter, American Medical Writers Association (President 1984-85); and Professional Writers of Cape Cod (President 1993-95). He was national correspondent for *The US Journal of Drug & Alcohol Dependence*.

At Boston's Channel 25, his show "It's Your Life" explored health and spirituality. He is a former CEO of Massachusetts Safety Council, and directed three other organizations. Working with the media, business, and government, he gained insight into the importance of building healthy relationships.

The author holds a BA degree *cum laude* from Boston College and an MA from The Graduate School, Boston University. He enjoys being a Secular Franciscan, Catholic Christian, and Unitarian.

Enlightening Reading...by Tom O'Connell
Health/Spirituality/Personal Growth/Recovery
<u>**Published by Sanctuary Unlimited**</u>
__**Danny The Prophet: A Fantastic Adventure**
An unforgettable novel about a man reluctant to be the last prophet. A trip into another dimension with a politician, a sage, an angel, perilous adventures, and divine revelations. ISBN 0-9620318-4-4

__**The Odd Duck:**
A Story for Odd People of All ages
A cheerful, inspiring fable for all "adult children." A lost duck raised in a chicken coop feels odd. After an identity crisis, she begins a quest for self-worth and healthy, lasting love. ISBN 0-9620318-3-6

__**Improving Intimacy: 10 Powerful Strategies**
A look at spiritually-based intimacy, with strategies for enhancing one's close relationships. Insights on addictive relating, control, listening, communication, conflict...and more. ISBN 0-9620318-2-8

__**Addicted? A Guide to Understanding Addiction**
A useful, practical, educational guide. Easy to read. Explains addiction's causes, effects, and recovery process. Covers alcohol, other drugs, food, gambling, sex. Gives useful tips. ISBN 0-9620318-0-1
Coming Soon...The Monadnock Revelations
A spiritual autobiography by Tom O'Connell.

Improving Intimacy 56

(Visit your local bookseller or use this order form)

www.sanctuary777.com
Sanctuary Unlimited
PO Box 25
Dennis Port MA 02639

Please send me the books I am listing below.
I expect delivery in 3-4 weeks.
Name:_____
Phone:_____
Address:_____
City:_____State:_____ZIP:_____

No. of Items	Title		Price
_____		$_____	
_____		$_____	
_____		$_____	
_____		$_____	
Total price_____		$_____	
Add $2.00 postage/hdlg first item____		$_____	
and $1.00 each additional item_____		$_____	
Mass. residents: add 5% sales tax____		$_____	
Enclose check/money order: Total		$_____	

(No cash or C.O.D., please)
Prices subject to change without notice.

Order online at amazon.com

Reader Opinion Survey

Please tear out this page, give us your comments, and forward to...
   Sanctuary Unlimited
   PO Box 25
   Dennisport, MA 02639

Subject: IMPROVING INTIMACY
Here are my comments on Tom O'Connell's book, *Improving Intimacy: (Please print or type)*

_____
_____
_____

(Please sign __and__ print your name)
Signed:_____

_____
Address:_____
City:_____State:_____Zip:_____
Occupation:_____

Please check one:
_____Yes, you may quote me for marketing and advertising, and in testimonial pages inserted into future copies of the book.

_____I request that you limit use of my comments to anonymous quotes such as "One reader said...."
Thank you for your cooperation.